Fuchsias

A Wisley Handbook

Fuchsias

GEORGE WELLS

Cassell

The Royal Horticultural Society

THE ROYAL HORTICULTURAL SOCIETY

Cassell Educational Limited
Villiers House, 41/47 Strand,
London WC2N 5JE
for the Royal Horticultural Society

First published 1971
New edition, fully revised and reset 1985
Second impression July 1985
Third impression June 1986
Fourth impression, revised July 1987
Fifth impression March 1988
Sixth impression March 1989
Third edition 1990

British Library Cataloguing in Publication Data
Wells, George
    Fuchsias. New ed.
    1. Fuchsias
    I. Title
    635.9′3344   SB413.F8

ISBN 0-304-32004-8

Line drawings by Peter Mennim
Photographs by Michael Warren

Typeset by Chapterhouse Ltd., Formby
Printed in Hong Kong by Wing King Tong Co. Ltd

Contents

History and uses 7
  As a plant in the house 8

Cultivation 12
  Potting: Composts, pots and potting 12
  Watering 18
  Feeding 20
  Summer pruning 20

Propagation 22
  Semi-hardwood cuttings 22
  Green tip cuttings in summer 22
  Short tip cuttings 25
  Green tip cuttings in spring 25
  By seed 26

Fuchsia breeding 27

Training 30
  Hanging basket 30
  Standard 31
  Pyramid 33

Overwintering 34

A selection of cultivars 36

Pests (by Andrew Halstead) 56

Diseases (by Audrey Brooks) 59

Growing fuchsias outdoors 61
  Hardy cultivars 63

History and uses

Although not a native of Britain the fuchsia always seems so British with its quiet charm and colouring, matching the country of its adoption in all its changing moods of sunshine and showers; a plant which has been taken to the heart of so many people. There are few who have not at some time or another admired or grown fuchsias, whether they are the owners of large gardens, or of just one or two plants in a small greenhouse or on a windowsill.

Some indication of this feeling lies in the fact that emigrants from this country must have carefully cherished a fuchsia plant among their meagre possessions as a reminder of the old country. No other explanation seems to account for the presence in North America, Australia and New Zealand of some of the older cultivars (varieties) which have been lost to cultivation in Britain.

Fuchsias are easy to grow, in pots or in the open, flowering continuously for a long period with a modest amount of attention. There is a wide range of flower colour from pure white to the extremes of violet in its most vivid tones, creams, yellow (in one species, *F. procumbens*), pinks of every hue and shade, from a barely perceptible tinge of deep rose and coral, reds through scarlets to the richest of carmines and crimsons of great intensity, delicate orange shades to deep turkey red underlaid with orange, and in many newly opened flowers, mauves, lavender, the richest of purples and even green.

In growth fuchsias may be found in the form of ground creeping plants to small trees. They can be trained to grow to almost any shape, such as standards or fans. Fuchsias can be grown to flower all the year round provided that the right conditions are maintained, although they do not flower very profusely during the short days of winter, and most people allow them to become dormant then. Even with the most modest equipment fuchsias will flower for four to eight months continuously. Outdoors they will flower for four to five months of summer and autumn.

The history of the fuchsia for the western world started in 1703 when Father Plumier, a missionary, published a description of a plant he called *Fuchsia triphylla flore coccinea*. For many years it was not known exactly where Plumier had collected this plant,

'Swingtime', a very adaptable fuchsia which is easy to grow

and it was not until 1873 when Thomas Hogg of New York sent home seeds from San Domingo that the home of the fuchsia became known. The name *Fuchsia* was derived from Leonard Fuchs, a German professor of botany, in whose honour the genus was named by Father Plumier.

The first plants to be introduced to Europe almost 200 years ago were *Fuchsia magellanica* and *F. coccinea*. They were followed a little later by *F. arborescens*, *F. microphylla* and *F. fulgens*. All of these are still grown today.

The first record of hybridization, in 1825, was between *F. arborescens* and *F. coccinea* and *F. macrostemma*, but it is not known what the progeny was like. Since then a great deal of hybridizing has been carried out in many countries using *F. magellanica* and *F. fulgens* as parents, among others, and as a result there are now many hundreds of hybrids of complex parentage.

The parents of the fuchsias that are grown today come from subtropical climates, being native to central and southern America and to New Zealand. In this country most fuchsias have to be grown with some protection, at least during the winter. There are places in the west of Britain where fuchsias have become almost naturalized, and hedges in flower are a familiar sight near the coast in summer. There are several fuchsia cultivars which are hardy enough to survive the winter outside in colder parts of Britain, but the cultivars must be chosen carefully and there are certain factors of cultivation advised. Fuchsias that are not hardy can be treated as summer bedding plants, being planted out in the open in summer, and then lifted for over-wintering in a frost-free store. Fuchsias are primarily plants for the greenhouse but they can also be grown in the house with little trouble.

AS A PLANT IN THE HOUSE

When thinking of growing a fuchsia indoors it is essential to choose a cultivar (variety) that will stand up to the difficult and dry conditions of a living room. Some are better able than others to retain their buds and flowers in spite of dry air conditions; others will drop their flowers immediately they are transferred to an atmosphere drier than that to which they have been accustomed. Often people buy plants from the local market and many of these are well suited as house plants. They are usually

'Brutus', above, and 'Lena', below, are both ideal as house plants

the hardy or semi-hardy cultivars that are easy to grow, such as 'Brutus', 'Alice Hoffman', 'Charming', 'Mrs Popple', 'Rose of Castille', 'Lena', 'Southgate', 'Tennessee Waltz' and 'Swingtime'.

When feeding plants indoors start with a weak liquid feed, this being one-third of the manufacturers suggested strength, once a fortnight. Increase the strength as the plant grows and flowers, to the full rate as recommended, weekly.

Syringing over the plant and the undersides of the leaves occasionally will benefit the plants, and also deter pests such as red spider mite.

From early autumn, even if it is flowering well, the plant should be gradually brought to dormancy by progressively reducing the amount of water given. If possible put the plant outside in a sunny position to ripen the wood, before storing it for the winter. A frost-free place should be chosen for overwintering, such as a garage, shed or cool cellar.

The plant should not be forgotten completely during the winter, but must be looked at about once a fortnight to check that the soil has not become dried out, and that the plant has not started to grow prematurely. If the soil is very dry it should be thoroughly moistened with tepid water; this damping should be enough for a few more weeks in the cellar. If the plant is showing early growth, the conditions are too warm. Move the plant to a cooler position, but still a frost-free one.

After winter, if the fuchsia is to be kept in the house, repot the plant, prune it (see p. 34) and place it in a light airy position to encourage new growth for the new season.

Below: 'Other Fellow', a free flowering bushy cultivar
Opposite: 'Lady Thumb', above, a fine hardy fuchsia; 'Tennessee Waltz', below, particularly recommended for beginners

Cultivation

POTTING

Composts.   For the best results when growing fuchsias in pots it is essential that a good soil is used so that the plant has adequate nutrients. On no account try to make do with soil from the garden, as the plants will not thrive as they should.

There are ready-made potting soils available (composts) which may or may not contain loam. Loam is the ideal horticultural soil, being intermediate in texture between the extremes of sand and clay, but unfortunately its quality can vary considerably. It is important to know whether a potting soil contains loam or not, because the techniques of cultivation are different with loam-based and with loamless composts.

The most commonly available loam-based composts are those made according to formulae worked out at the John Innes Institute. These are the John Innes (J.I.) composts, of which there are four: one for seed sowing (J.I. seed) and three for potting which vary mainly in their fertilizer contents and are intended for progressively older plants. J.I. 1 is for rooted cuttings, and J.I. 2

'Peewee Rose', a vigorous fast-growing fuchsia for the garden

and J.I. 3 for plants in larger pots in which they are to spend most of their growing period. J.I. seed compost can be used for rooting cuttings, but many gardeners prefer to make their own mixture (see p. 16).

The J.I. composts are a mixture of loam with peat and sand. If one wants to make one's own composts these are the ingredients to obtain. The loam is made from turves, the top 4 or 5 inches of soil and grass from a well-grazed pasture; these are stacked grass side down and left to rot for about 6 months. Prepared loam can be bought in but it should be seen before buying. All loam should be sterilized before using, to prevent transmission of any soil-borne diseases.

Peat for horticulture is granulated sphagnum peat, which is sold in bags and bales of up to 2 cwt. When delivered it is often dry and must be thoroughly dampened before use. Spread out a quantity on the floor and water it well using a watering can with a sprinkler so that the water is distributed fairly evenly. Turn the peat, water again and then add another layer of peat. Repeat the process and mix the peat well. If possible leave it for 24 hours before using, so that it is evenly damp.

Leaf-mould can be used as an alternative to peat if available. It must be made from good clean beech or oak leaves which have been stacked and kept damp while rotting for about a year. After that, it should be possible to knock the leaves to pieces with a fork. Leaf-mould should be passed through a sieve of 3/8-inch mesh, before using. Like loam, it should be sterilized before use.

The best types of sand to use are coarse river sand or a good sharp Bedfordshire silver sand. Fine washed pit sand used by builders is not suitable as it tends to turn to a solid mass when wet.

Loamless composts. In recent years several types of compost have been developed which do not contain any loam. These were developed because loam can be such a variable material, in pH (a measure of acidity or alkalinity) and texture among other things, so that the expected performance of the plants was not always obtained. Another advantage of loamless composts is that the ingredients do not need to be sterilized before use.

There are several recipes for loamless composts, some contain peat only, others contain peat and sand, but with both, major nutrients and some trace elements are added. Fuchsias will grow just as well in loamless composts as in loam-based types, but there are two important factors to remember. First nutrition.

The loamless composts generally contain a lower nutrient content than the loam-based ones, particularly of minor elements.

Above: 'Trase', one of the best hardy fuchsias
Opposite: 'Cliffs Hardy', above, a compact, medium-sized plant for
outdoors; 'Red Spider', below, with long flowers and trailing growth

The supply of nitrogen also needs to be watched and one must start feeding earlier to be sure that vegetative growth (for which nitrogen is needed) does not slow down. Young plants or those recently re-potted into fresh compost will not require feeding. When plants are growing well and the soil is beginning to fill with new roots feeding should start as mentioned before with the weak feed, increasing in strength and frequency as plants progress.

There is a large choice of feeds e.g. Maxicrop. Vitafeed 101, and Phostrogen; these have all the required nutrients for healthy plants.

The other main difference is the watering technique. It is very important that the peat composts never dry out because they are then very difficult to re-wet properly. Overwatering is just as bad because the composts become compacted and sodden, and without oxygen the roots soon rot.

Loamless composts are lighter in weight than loam-based ones which is an advantage when carrying the pots. However, a well-grown fuchsia in a peat compost may become top-heavy, particularly if it is a standard grown in a plastic pot, and the shoots are easily damaged if the plant is knocked over. The very open texture of the peat compost means that it is difficult to insert a stake firmly. Taking into regard these last two points it is better to use a loam-based compost when growing a large plant such as a standard.

14

Pots. Both clay and plastic types are easily available, and gardeners have their preferences. Fuchsias will grow well in both types, but there are some differences in soil conditions in each type.

The chief advantage of clay pots is that they absorb moisture, and so the chance of damaging the plant by overwatering the plants is less. I have noticed that in clay pots the roots are slower to reach the bottom than in plastic pots, as they seem to travel round the sides before reaching the drainage hole. In plastic pots the roots often arrive sooner at the drainage holes at the bottom of the pot.

Compost mixtures and potting. With loam-based composts the proportions of ingredients are varied according to the age of the plant to be potted. A standard mixture for seeds is 2 parts loam, 1 part peat and 1 part sand, mixed together evenly and with 1 oz. superphosphate added per bushel. Alternatively J.I. seed compost may be used.

Cuttings need an open-textured medium to encourage root growth, and a good mixture is 1 part of peat with 1 part of silver sand. Little or no extra nutrients are needed for cuttings. (Details of taking different types of cuttings are given on pp. 22–26).

The next stage is to pot up the rooted cuttings, and the ingredients of J.I. No. 1 are 7 parts loam, 3 parts peat and 2 parts silver sand. J.I. base fertilizer (containing hoof and horn, super-phosphate of lime and sulphate of potash*) is added at 4 oz per bushel of the mixture. An alternative is Vitax Q4 which also contains trace elements. When potting rooted cuttings use a 3-inch pot (diameter at the top). If using loam-based compost and a clay pot, put one or two bits of broken pot (crocks) over the drainage hole and then about ½ inch of peat for drainage. Fill the pot half-full with compost, and firm it down gently. Sit the rooted cutting on this and fill the pot with more compost, firming it down lightly but leaving a space about ½ to ¾ inch below the rim of the pot, to allow room for watering.

The same technique is used with a loamless compost although the extra layer of peat above the drainage hole is not necessary. With plastic pots there are generally several small drainage holes which do not need to be crocked as the peat is not likely to fall through.

The next stage is to transfer the plants to a larger pot (i.e. 3-inch to 5-inch) allowing more room for root growth, adding some new

*The appropriate nutrient analysis is 5% nitrogen, 7.2% phosphoric acid and 9.7% potash.

soil at the same time. The same mixture (J.I. No. 1) is used as for the first potting and new soil added in the gap between the pot wall and the unbroken soil ball, firming it down with the fingers, but allowing 1 inch space at the top for watering.

The final potting is into 7- or 8-inch pots. If mixing one's own compost the proportions are 7 parts of coarse loam, 3 parts of peat and 2 parts of sand or grit, plus 12 oz J.I. base fertilizer per bushel. J.I. 3 is the ready-made alternative.

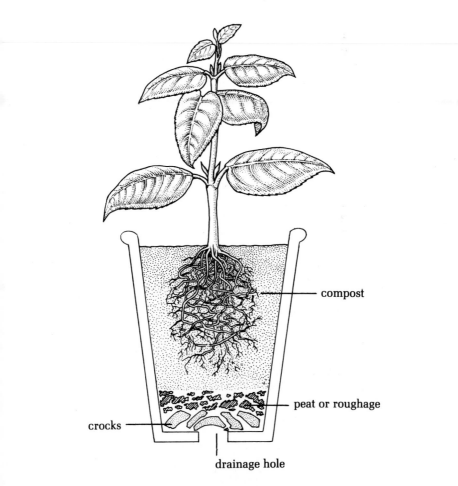

A fuchsia that has been potted on into a clay pot. Note the space between the rim of the pot and the soil – this allows plenty of room for water.

When potting into these larger pots leave 1½ inches space below the rim for watering. The plant will be in the pot for several weeks and the mass of roots formed sometimes forces up the soil level so reducing the amount of water that can be applied.

Loamless (peat-based) composts are available prepared for cuttings and seeds, and for potting. With a peat-based compost the nutrient content at the final potting is not likely to be sufficient for several months of growth, and so regular feeding with a nutrient solution must start early.

For potting, the compost should be moist but not wet. The test is to squeeze a handful, and if, on being released, it falls apart, it is too dry. If it remains a solid mass, it is too wet. The right texture is when the compost adheres, but crumbles easily when touched. When firming the soil in the pot it should not be compacted round the roots, but it should be pressed firmly around the plant to hold it securely in the pot.

WATERING

One of the most difficult questions to answer is 'How often should I water my plants?' There is no short answer: it all depends on the conditions of the day. When the sun is shining the plants are taking up and giving off much more water than on a dull, cloudy day. So the water requirement varies from day to day depending

The well known and reliable 'Princess Dollar'

'Pink Marshmallow' has exceptionally large flowers

on the plant's situation. It also depends on whether plants are growing in clay or plastic pots (see p. 16).

When fuchsias are in active growth the plants should be checked at least once a day, preferably twice if the weather is hot and sunny. It is possible to tell whether a plant in a clay pot needs water by tapping it with a tapper made from bamboo cane with a wooden cotton reel at its head. Tap gently at least half-way down the pot and if the pot sounds hollow it needs watering; if there is a dull ring no water is required. The tapper is not effective with plastic pots and with these one must test the weight of the pot to discover whether it needs water. If one waters a plant well and compares it with an unwatered plant it is quite easy to judge the difference between a wet and a dry plant.

When water is given fill the pot to its rim. If only driblets of water are given the bottom half of the pot never gets properly wet.

If the water does not soak through the pot pour it off, knock out the soil ball and check the drainage. It is possible that a worm has clogged the drainage hole. Tap the soil ball on one side and the worm will probably emerge.

FEEDING

The main need of the fuchsia is for a feed containing the three main nutrients, nitrogen, phosphorus and potassium (for shoot growth, root growth and flowering, respectively) in balanced proportions. These are incorporated in the composts before potting but they are gradually used up and extra regular feeding is needed throughout the summer.

In a loam-based compost it is generally not necessary to start feeding until the plants are in flower in their final pots (7-inch). Plants in loamless composts are likely to need feeding when they are still in smaller pots, probably in 5-inch pots.

Application of a diluted liquid feed from a watering can is the easiest method, giving it regularly once a fortnight to a plant in a loam-based compost, and once a week to one in a peat-based compost.

SUMMER PRUNING

In order to get a well-shaped plant some pinching out of the shoots or 'summer pruning' is needed. A bush shape is probably the most usual form. The growth of side branches is induced by pinching out the main shoot which would otherwise grow taller and taller making a long, thin plant.

The main shoot of a young plant is pinched out when three or four pairs of leaves have formed. The side shoots in the axils of these leaves are thus stimulated into growth and are pinched again after two more pairs of leaves have formed. There is no need to do any more summer pruning for the simple bush shape, otherwise flowering will be delayed. Flowering starts about six weeks after the second pinching.

This method relates to plants raised from cuttings, with one central shoot. With second-season plants or older, where there is already a branch system, this is cut back in spring before growth starts, so that later probably only one pinching will be needed, at two or three pairs of leaves.

For more elaborate training systems see pp. 30–33.

'Rufus the Red', a strong grower and prolific flowerer

Propagation

The fuchsia is a plant that will root with the greatest of ease, which is probably why it is so popular. The method normally used is propagation by cuttings, and this is so easy that other methods of vegetative propagation are hardly used. Cuttings are taken at different times of the year according to the equipment available for overwintering and conditions for rooting.

There are various kinds of propagators on the market which can be used for rooted cuttings. These are pots or boxes which have a firm plastic 'hood' and sometimes a simple system of heating from below. They are very suitable for rooting small quantities of cuttings.

SEMI-HARDWOOD CUTTINGS

This is the most convenient method for those who do not have a heated greenhouse.

The cuttings are taken late in the season, when the bark at the base of the shoots has started to harden or ripen for the winter. The cuttings are taken in September, October or even later, and are kept in a frost-free place during the winter while rooting.

Select side shoots of from 4 to 6 inches long (10–15 cm), and pull them off so that a piece of the main stem is still attached to the base of the cutting. This is known as the 'heel' and rooting is accelerated by leaving it at the base of the shoot. Trim the heel with a sharp knife or razor blade, and insert the cutting round the edge of a 3- or 4-inch pot (see page 26). The pots are then put into a box that is deep enough just to bury the rim. The box is filled with sand, ashes or wood fibre and the pots inserted into this: the boxes and pots are thoroughly watered and put in a frost-free greenhouse or frame for the winter. By putting the pots in a box partly filled with sand the environment for rooting is maintained at uniform level, and this factor is important for good rooting. By the spring a root system will have been formed and the young plants can be potted off.

GREEN TIP CUTTINGS IN SUMMER

These can be taken in mid-August, selecting shoots that are about 3 inches long (7.5cm) with two or three pairs of leaves. Cut the

Using a razor blade to take cuttings.

shoots just below the point where the lowest pair of leaves joins the stem and cut off these two leaves. Insert the cuttings, 2 inches apart, in a box 2½ inches deep (5cm × 6cm), into a compost of 1 part loam, 1 part peat and 3 parts of sand. Drainage crocks are placed in the bottom of the box as the plants are to remain in the same soil throughout the winter. Place the box of cuttings in a cold frame or greenhouse, water and shade during the day if necessary. The cuttings should have rooted within about 3 weeks, and they can then be given more ventilation and light.

As soon as the frosts come remove the cuttings to a frost-free position and keep the plants just moist during the winter. The cuttings will probably lose all their leaves, but when the weather improves about February they will start to grow again. They are then carefully taken from their boxes and potted into 3-inch pots, soon making nice plants.

I prefer to take cuttings in late July or early August, but for such cuttings one must be able to maintain a minimum temperature of 55°F. (13°C.) in the greenhouse during the winter. The same sort of shoots are taken as described above and inserted into 3-inch pots, one of which will take four cuttings. A suitable compost is 1 part peat to 1 part silver sand. Then the pots are placed in a closed propagating case in the greenhouse, shading as required. A propagating case can be made from a fairly deep wooden box with a sheet of glass or plastic film over the top.

These cuttings will root in 2 or 3 weeks. Then gradually more ventilation is given and as soon as they are hardened off the rooted cuttings are potted singly into 3-inch pots using J.I. No. 1. There is one intermediate potting before the winter, into 5-inch pots, and the final potting is done in February. These plants should be flowering in May, and can be kept in flower until September with good cultivation.

Increases in heating costs in the last few years mean that it is now very expensive to maintain high minimum winter temperatures in greenhouses. It is still possible to grow plants to a very

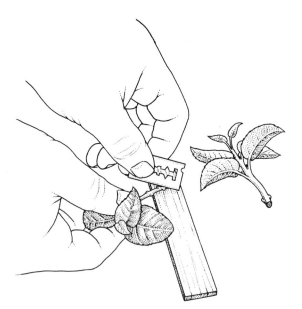

Using a razor blade to trim cuttings.

good standard at lower temperatures. If a minimum temperature of 50°F. (10°C.) can be maintained in the winter take the cuttings in the first half of July. With a temperature of 45–47°F. (7–8°C.) take the cuttings in mid-June. The final potting can still be in January or early February giving as high a temperature as possible (up to 60°F. or 15°C.) after potting.

Green tip cuttings can also be taken in spring (see below).

SHORT TIP CUTTINGS

The third type of cutting is taken early in the season from plants which have been newly started into growth.

The overwintered plants are pruned back early in the year (January to March), by cutting off all green shoots of the previous season's growth, into the brown-barked (ripened) wood. The plants are kept at a temperature of 60 to 65°F. (15 to 18°C.), and syringed once or twice a day to induce the dormant buds to shoot. Too much water should not be given as overwatering can easily kill old plants. When the new young shoots have produced three pairs of leaves, they are cut off with a sharp knife or razor blade, taking two pairs of leaves, but leaving one pair behind from which two more shoots will be produced.

This cutting needs no trimming and is inserted at the edge of a 3-inch pot, with three other cuttings. The compost given on p. 16 is used and the cuttings inserted so that they are just held up by the soil. After planting, each pot is labelled, watered and placed in a closed propagating case. The glass may be shaded if necessary, and at first air is allowed for only a short period each day (about ½ hour). The cuttings should root in about 10 to 14 days; after that more and more ventilation can be given before the rooted cuttings are potted up.

GREEN TIP CUTTINGS IN SPRING

These are treated in the same way as the short-tip cuttings. They are shaded as necessary, watered and gradually ventilated. These cuttings are ideal for summer bedding if potted on as soon as rooted, grown in a warm greenhouse i.e. 10 to 13°C (50–55°F). Pinch out the growing tip at four pairs of leaves; this should result in six to eight breaks and these may be allowed to flower. If a more bushy plant is required stop again at two or three pairs of leaves, the resulting shoots will be shorter but will flower at the end of June or early July and for the rest of the summer.

Another method of treating cuttings is to put the cuttings in the pot inside a large polythene bag. Wire half-loops are inserted in the pot so that the bag does not fall in on the cuttings, which could result in rotting. The top of the bag is closed so that it is airtight. The bag is opened when ventilation is needed, as one would do with a frame. Those who have no greenhouse but cold frames can root their fuchsia cuttings in these, but such cuttings cannot be taken until the middle of April at the earliest, and rooting is slower than in the warmer greenhouse.

Left: Several short tip or green tip cuttings can be inserted at the edge of a 3-inch pot.

Right: Cuttings about to be covered with a plastic bag.

PROPAGATION BY SEED

Few fuchsias are raised from seed except by breeders, because, to perpetuate a hybrid, taking cuttings is the only method to produce a plant with exactly the same characteristics as its parents.

Fuchsias are nevertheless easy to raise from seed, and in greenhouses when the pots are standing on a layer of damp gravel on the bench, seedlings are often found, having sown themselves in the gravel.

Fuchsia breeding

Many people are interested in this side of fuchsia growing but are a little confused as to what is required. The first essential is the ability to recognise a good cultivar.

The first crosses made are usually fact finding ones to establish the type of parent for the future. Many good ones have been produced more by chance than intent. Only by experimental crosses can a breeding programme begin.

The first thing is to select your favourite cultivars which display vigorous, healthy growth and free flowering characteristics. Pollinating is a fairly simple operation if one follows a few simple rules.

Like most other flowers the fuchsia has stamens and pistil and can fertilise itself, so that is where rule one applies. This part is known as emasculation, i.e. removal of stamens. Select the flower to be used when it is about to open naturally, open the flower fully and remove the stamens with a small pair of scissors: a little difficulty may present itself with fully double flowers as they sometimes restrict the complete emergence of the anthers, therefore remove the petals carefully, this eases the process of emasculation.

Pollen from the male member must be fresh and is then transferred to the prepared flower by taking the anther with its pollen and applying direct to the stigma; as the stigma is not always fully receptive at this stage, make sure a supply of pollen is left thereon and fertilisation will take place when the stigma is ripe.

Successful pollination is governed to a large degree by temperature, 70° to 75°F. (21°–24°C.) is the ideal for optimum success. The pollinated flower must be protected from other pollen drifting in the atmosphere or from insects, so cover with a muslin bag, enclose the whole flower, and leave the fruit to ripen. Do not expect all crosses to be successful, there are many disappointments for the hybridiser. The main reason for failure is the inability of the pollen tube to find the right organic nutrient to sustain continuous growth down the style to the embryo sac, this is where the subsequent development takes place.

Reciprocal crosses, i.e. crosses between two plants on which the roles of male and female are reversed, are often practised, but it makes little difference to the character of the resulting seedlings. The only advantage for this practice is that the pollen germination is sometimes more effective than the other way round. Always keep clear records of each cross made.

From here one waits until the skin of the fruits begin to show signs of shrivelling. They are then suitable for picking and cleaning. Remove the flesh and skin and wash lightly in some water: when washing, the good seeds will sink to the bottom of the receptacle. The seeds are then dried in the air. Be sure to label them. Seeds may be sown at any time, but probably the early spring is best, the resulting seedlings will usually flower the first year. Sow in clean well-drained pans in a good seed compost either with or without loam, place in a propagating case and shade from the sun until seedlings appear. Do not overwater. As soon as they are large enough to handle pot into 2 or 2½-inch (2–6cm) pots, always make sure labels with all details are replaced with each batch. As soon as they are growing away remove to cooler conditions 50° to 55°F. (11°–13°C.)

The general ancestry of present day fuchsias is so remote it is only possible to guess at the results of crossing individual cultivars, however an understanding of the basic laws of inheritance will help the art of breeding new cultivars. One will often find the best results are obtained by back crossing seedlings on to either parents thus obtaining the best qualities of both parents. If one is looking for pastel shades use one parent with white in its make-up on the stronger coloured cultivars.

Below: 'Prelude', a hardy fuchsia
Opposite: 'Keystone', above, a delightful small cultivar; 'Chillerton Beauty', below, a tall plant for garden or greenhouse

Training

The ordinary bush form is the most usual shape in which fuchsias are grown, and details of the summer pruning technique to obtain this have been given earlier (p. 20). But there are more complicated forms to which the fuchsia plant can be trained, and some details of how to obtain these are given below.

HANGING BASKET

A cultivar to be used for this should be chosen for its cascading habit of growth, e.g. 'Eden Beauty', 'Henri Poincare'. The same method of pinching as for the bush form is used. A suitable basket (usually of wire, although plastic is now also used) is lined with a layer of moss or polythene, filling it with compost, such as the J.I.3 mixture. Plant firmly and water in, allowing the branches to hang over the side of the basket. With plants that have been grown through the winter, one good-sized plant is enough for one basket. The baskets are made up in February and grown at 55° to 60°F. (13° to 16°C.). Plants in baskets need to be watered every day, especially in cases where overhanging eaves prevent rain from reaching them.

'Lena', 'Swingtime' and 'Tennessee Waltz' show the merits of fuchsias in hanging baskets

STANDARD

When selecting plants to be grown as standards, it is worth looking for those which have three leaves at a joint instead of the more usual two. This character is sometimes varietal, sometimes a result of climatic conditions, but in a group of twenty fuchsias one can hope to find 3 or 4 plants with these 3-leaf opposites. With such a plant three shoots will break after each stopping instead of two, so making a bushier head, so it is worth while taking extra time to look for these plants.

If one knows the total height of the standard required, one must remember that the head when complete will add 11 to 15 inches (30–37cm) to the top of the stem from the position of the first stopping (pinching). For a standard 4½ feet (1.4m) tall, the first stopping is therefore done at about 3½ feet (92–106cm).

After the first stopping when the side shoots are seen to be developing satisfactorily in the axils of the top three sets of leaves,

Left: a shoot showing three-leaf opposites. Right: removing side shoots, but leaving the basal leaves.

any side shoots appearing lower down the main stem are removed. The basal leaves are not removed when taking away the side shoots. These will remain on the plant after the plants are in flower, thus helping the development of the plant by drawing up the nutrients from the pot.

Suitable cultivars for standards are 'Beverley', 'Checkerboard', 'Sleigh Bells', 'Billy Green', 'Hidcote Beauty', 'White Queen', 'Maharaja', 'The Aristocrat', 'My Fair Lady', 'Television', and 'Party Frock'.

PYRAMID

An upright single-stem plant is selected and grown until the main stem is about 2½ feet tall (75cm). At this height the tip is removed

'Trail Blazer', a vigorous trailer with a profusion of flowers

allowing the side shoots below to develop. These are then stopped at two or three pairs of leaves, but allowing the topmost upright shoot to continue to grow upwards for a further 12 to 15 inches (30–37cm). Then the tip is removed again allowing more side shoots to develop, which are then stopped at two or three pairs of leaves. This process is repeated until the required height is reached. It may take two years to produce a well-shaped plant.

Suitable cultivars for pyramids are 'Molesworth', 'Ting-a-Ling', 'Hindu Belle', 'Lady Kathleen Spence', 'Jack Acland', 'Temptation' and 'Uncle Charlie'.

'Checkerboard' makes an excellent standard

Overwintering

One way of keeping plants going from year to year is by taking cuttings. But fuchsias can also be kept for several years by making the plants dormant and storing them in this dormant state in a frost-free place for the winter.

To induce the plants to become dormant watering is gradually reduced in September and October until growth stops. If possible during this period, the plants should be put outside in the sun during the day, to help harden (ripen) the bark on the shoots. Well ripened shoots are less likely to die back during the winter storage period than are green shoots.

The plants are then put in a frost-free place for the winter, and looked at about every two weeks to make sure that the soil in the pot is still moist. If it is too dry, thoroughly soak the soil with tepid water, which should be sufficient for several more weeks.

If there is any sign of premature growth, then the atmosphere is too warm, and the plants should be removed somewhere cooler, but still frost free.

Early in the spring the plants are brought out and pruned back to one or two buds per shoot. All weak and crossing shoots are

'Coralle', a bush plant with unusual flowers and foliage

'Eva Boerg', a gracefully arching fuchsia for the border or a large pot

removed at this time too, so that the plant is a reasonably open shape. Knock out the plant from the pot and remove as much of the old soil as possible, and then repot into a pot that will just take the root ball, using J.I. No. 1 compost.

The plant is then put in a greenhouse or other warm place and syringed once or twice a day. The pot should not be watered until the plant starts into growth, because it is easy to kill plants by overwatering at this stage. Once growth starts water sparingly until the shoots are growing vigorously. Then the new shoots can be stopped, to increase the size of the head. When the pots are full of roots the plants are repotted into 7- or 8-inch pots using J.I. No. 3 compost.

This method of overwintering is satisfactory for those who are not able to keep the fuchsias in a warm enough temperature (50°F., 10°C.). Plants will continue to grow for many years with overwintering, but unfortunately the flowers gradually get smaller. The time does come when it is better to start again with new plants raised from cuttings.

A selection of cultivars

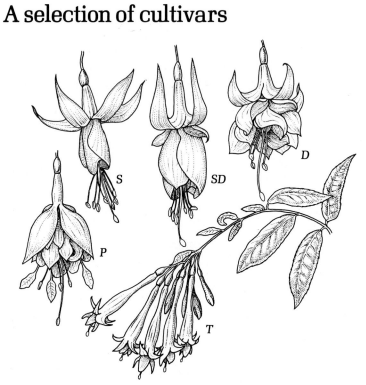

The different flower types of fuchsia hybrids.

KEY to line drawing and list of cultivars.

D.	=	Double flowers.
S.	=	Single flowers.
S.D.	=	Semi-double flowers.
T.	=	*Triphylla* hybrids; all these have long tubes, short sepals, and small single corollas.
P.	=	flower showing petaloids.
*F.	=	Coloured foliage.

*most of these will grow best in shady positions, as bright sunshine tends to scorch the parts of the leaves with light markings.

N.B. In the list of cultivars opposite, the raiser's name is given in brackets. Hardy, half-hardy and tender cvs. are listed here in alphabetical order, and a further list of cvs. that have been given awards for hardiness is on pages 63–64.

CULTIVARS

Abbé Farges S.D. (Lemoine 1901, France) Tube and sepals pale cherry red, corolla rosy lilac. Small flowers in abundance on upright growth.

Achievement S. (Melville 1886, U.K.) Tube and sepals carmine, corolla reddish purple, scarlet at base. A good hardy fuchsia, makes a good show plant. Easy to grow and very free flowering.

Alaska D. (Schnabel 1963, S.A.) Tube white, sepals white tipped green, corolla white. Strong growing, self branching cultivar. Free flowering. Largest and purest white flowers obtained by growing in greenhouse. Easy to grow.

Alice Ashton D. (Tiret 1971, U.S.A.) Tube pale pink, sepals pink, paler at tip, then green, deep pink underneath, corolla porcelain blue, pink at base. A very pretty trailing cultivar.

Alice Hoffman S. (Kleise 1911, Germany) Tube and sepals cerise pink with white corolla. The small flowers are freely produced. Growth compact.

Angels Flight D. (Martin 1957, U.S.A.) Tube white to pale pink, sepals pink, deeper at base and edge, corolla white, veined pale pink. A vigorous growing, self branching fuchsia. Can be grown as bush or trailer.

Angela Leslie D. (Tiret 1959, U.S.A.) Tube and sepals pink, corolla bright pink. Large flowers freely produced. Makes a well shaped plant, either bush or standard.

Anthea Day D. (J. Day 1981, U.K.) Tube and sepals rich waxy red, corolla blush pink. An easy grower. Good upright bush. This seedling from 'Pink Cloud' × 'Pink Quartet' flowers freely over a long period.

Avocet S. (Travis 1958, U.K.) Tube and sepals red, corolla white veined red. Vigorous and very free flowering. Excellent as a standard.

Avon Gem S. (J. Lockyer 1978, U.K.) Tube and sepals red, narrow corolla purple to magenta. Medium-sized blooms. Vigorous grower, very free flowering. Makes a good bush or standard.

Avon Gold S. (Lockyer 1985, U.K.) Tube pale pink, sepals pink tipped green, corolla pale lavender pink. Medium-sized flowers produced in abundance. The foliage is beautifully variegated cream and gold. Makes a strong shapely bush. Excellent for showing.

Balkon S. (Balkonigen). (Neubronner 1914, Germany) Tube pale pink, sepals pale pink, tipped green, deeper pink underneath, corolla pink. This is a fuchsia which cascades straight down from the sides of a basket, with a lot of trailing growth. Must be grown well, will then repay with profuse bloom. It pays to plant several in each basket.

Barbara S. (Tolley 1973, U.K.) Tube pale pink, sepals pink, deeper pink underneath, corolla cherry pink. Growth upright. Free flowering.

Beauty of Bath S.D. (Colville 1965, U.K.) Tube pale pink, sepals pale pink, deeper at base, edged bright pink, tipped green, corolla white. Upright growth, quite free branching. Flowers well.

Bella Forbes D. (Dobbie Forbes 1890, U.K.) Tube and sepals cerise, corolla creamy white, lightly veined cerise. This is an outstanding fuchsia. It grows rather upright, but bushes well, before flowering, which is very free.

Beverley S. (R. Holmes 1975, U.K.) Tube pink, sepals pink tipped green, corolla bright magenta pink, light pink at base. Flowers profusely. Good as a standard.

Biddy Lester S. (R. Holmes 1984, U.K.) Tube and sepals neyron rose tipped green, corolla deep mallow purple. Self-branching, short jointed growth. Free flowering. A good standard and show cultivar.

Billy Green T. (Engels 1966) Flowers geranium lake. This is a vigorous grower, tall and upright, very suitable for standard. Very free flowering. (See page 39).

Blanche Regina D. (Clyne 1974, U.K.) Tube and sepals white, corolla violet, ageing to purple, flushed pink at base. Very vigorous cascade plant. Flowers profusely borne over a long period. Easy to grow.

Blue Gown D. (Milne, U.K.) Tube and sepals scarlet, corolla bluish purple, splashed pink and carmine. Growth vigorous, flowers freely. Good as a bush.

Blue Mink S. (R. Holmes 1975, U.K.) Tube bright carmine pink, sepals carmine, corolla dense blue purple, pink at base, veined carmine. This is a superb cultivar, makes an excellent bushy plant covered freely with flowers.

Blue Pinwheel S. (Stubbs 1970, U.S.A.) Tube and sepals rose pink, corolla lavender blue, pale pink at base, veined rose. Very good basket cultivar.

Blush of Dawn D. (Martin 1962, U.S.A.) Tube greenish white, sepals white, tipped green, corolla pale silvery lilac, pale pink at base. Excellent grower in all forms.

Bouquet D. (Rozain-Boucharat 1893, France) Tube and sepals carmine, corolla violet, ageing to reddish purple. Growth is upright, dwarf and bushy. A lovely miniature fuchsia. Very free flowering. Makes a very nice standard.

Bridesmaid D. (Tiret 1952, U.S.A.) Tube white, sepals white with pink flush, corolla pale lilac. Prolific, with good sized flowers. Good as a bush or half-standard.

Brutus S. (Lemoine 1897, France) Tube and sepals cherry red, corolla purple becoming lighter towards the base. Free flowering, medium-sized flowers. Vigorous growth. (See page 9).

Burning Bush F. (Courcelles) Tube red, sepals red, corolla reddish purple. Single. Foliage variegated, coppery red, yellow and green. Growth trailing, but rather stiff. Late flowering.

Cara Mia S.D. (Schnabel 1957, U.S.A.) Tube and sepals pale rose pink, corolla crimson. Flowers medium large. Prolific flowering. Cascade type of growth.

Caroline S. (Miller 1967, U.K.) Tube and sepals cream flushed pink, corolla opening pale pink, maturing to cyclamen. Good grower.

Cascade S. (Dr J.B. Lagen, 1937.) Tube and sepals white with pink flush, recurving, corolla deep crimson. Flowers long and pendulous, very freely produced. One of the best for baskets.

Charlie Girl D. (Tanfield 1970, U.K.) Tube pink, sepals rose pink, corolla lilac blue, paler at base, veined rose. Strong upright growth, ideal as standard, has a nice branching habit. Free flowering.

Charming S. (Lye 1895, U.K.) Tube and sepals carmine red, corolla red-purple. Medium-sized flowers. Very easy to grow.

Checkerboard S. (Weekes and Jones 1948. U.S.A.) Tube pink, sepals white, corolla red. Very free flowering. Upright growth. Excellent as standard. (See page 33).

Opposite: 'Billy Green', excellent for training as a standard

China Doll D. (Tiret 1956, U.S.A.) Tube and sepals red, non reflexing sepals, corolla white. Large distinctive flower. Excellent grower as bush or standard.

China Lantern S. (Unknown origin, probably U.S.A.) Tube bright pink, sepals white, corolla rose pink. Makes a very bushy plant. Flowers freely produced.

Citation S. (Hodges 1953, U.S.A.) Tube and sepals pale rose, corolla white, pinkish at base. The corolla is formed in an unusual spreading manner, with recurved segments. (See page 43).

Cliff's Unique D. (Gadsby 1974, U.K.) Tube and sepals waxy white, corolla pale blue. Medium-sized flowers produced in profusion. A first-class all-purpose cultivar.

Cloth of Gold F. (Stafford 1863.) Tube dark pink, sepals pinkish red, corolla purple. S or S.D. Foliage golden ageing to green flushed bronze. Lax upright growth. (See page 42).

Coachman S. (Bright, U.K.) Tube and sepals salmon pink, corolla orange vermilion. Self branching so needs very little attention. Flowers freely, makes excellent standard but can also be trained in a basket. (See opposite).

Constellation D. (Schnabel 1957, U.S.A.) Tube white, sepals white, tipped green, corolla creamy white. One of the most free flowering white cultivars on a well shaped plant. Easy to grow and makes a first class standard, probably the best double white.

Coralle or **Koralle** T. (Bondstedt 1906) Flowers orange, foliage blue-green. Free flowering over long period. Suitable only as a bush plant. (See page 34).

Countess of Maritza D. (Holmes 1977, U.K.) Sepals pale pink, broad and long, tube short, corolla lilac. Attractive flowers freely produced on bushy upright growth.

Cross Check S. (Brouwer 1985, Netherlands) Tube and sepals pink, corolla rich purple. The medium-sized flowers contrast well with the deep golden yellow foliage. Free flowering, excellent as bush or standard.

Crystal Blue S.D. (Kennett 1962, U.S.A.) Tube greenish white, sepals white tipped green, corolla violet blue, white at base. A very pretty blue and white cultivar. Easy to grow. Blooms very freely and makes a good bushy plant.

Curtain Call D. (Munkner 1961, U.S.A.) Tube white, sepals white, flushed pink underneath, corolla rich rosy cerise, white at base. Quite large flowers produced profusely on an easy to grow plant. May be grown as a standard, bush and trailer.

Dancing Flame D. (Stubbs 1981, U.S.A.) Tube, sepals and outer corolla various shades of orange, inner part of corolla carmine. An easy-to-grow first-class cultivar suitable for all purposes.

David Lockyer D. (Holmes 1968, U.K.) Tube white, sepals white, flushed pink underneath, tipped green, corolla crimson, some petals splashed or striped white. Growth upright. The flower is unusual in that it produces a secondary skirt from the centre of the corolla. Makes a bush or standard.

Day by Day F. (Wagtails 1971, U.K.) Tube scarlet, sepals scarlet lighter at tips, corolla rosy purple. Single. Foliage variegated, green, cream and cerise. A sport from 'Emile Zola'. Upright but bushy growth.

Doreen Stroud D. (Stroud 1988, U.K.) Tube and sepals light red, corolla deep lavender blue. A good bush but most useful in a hanging basket.

Dusky Rose D. (Waltz 1960, U.S.A.) Tube deep pink, sepals pink, corolla raspberry rose. Free flowering. Excellent trailer.

'Coachman' is self-branching but can also be trained as a standard or for a hanging basket

Dutch Mill S. (1960, U.S.A.)   Tube and sepals pale rose, corolla pale violet shading to white at base. A perfectly shaped flower. Free flowering.

Eden Beauty S. (Holmes 1973, U.K.)   Tube scarlet, sepals scarlet tipped green, corolla purple. Small foliage. Cascade type of growth so ideal for baskets.

Ellen Morgan D. (Holmes 1974, U.K.)   Tube salmon pink, sepals salmon pink, tipped green, corolla rich magenta, salmon pink at base. Makes a large strong growing plant. Easy to grow and very free flowering over a long period.

English Rose D. (Pacey 1987, U.K.)   Tube and sepals white, corolla light purple. Large well shaped flowers freely produced on good upright bushy growth. Should make a good standard.

Eva Boerg S.D. (Yorke 1943, U.K.)   Tube greenish white, sepals pinkish white, tipped green, pink underneath, corolla pinkish purple, paling at base and splashed pink. Rather lax upright growth, but is hardy. (See page 35).

Evensong S. (Colville 1968, U.K.)   Tube pink, sepals white tipped green, corolla white. Easy to grow. Good greenhouse plant. Very free flowering.

Falling Stars S. (Reiter 1941, U.S.A.)   Tube pale pinkish red, sepals reddish pink, salmon underneath, tipped green, corolla dusky reddish orange. Most unusual

'Cloth of Gold', a fuchsia notable for its foliage

coloured corolla, when fully grown really striking; looks almost brown. Flowers are freely produced and this cultivar makes an excellent standard.

Fiona S. (Clarke 1962, U.K.) Tube white, sepals white tipped green, corolla blue ageing to reddish purple, with a white flash at the base. Flowers freely borne. Good as bush or standard.

Forward Look S. (Gadsby 1973, U.K.) Tube pink, sepals pink tipped green, corolla bluish violet. Good upright growth. Flowers profusely.

Freeland Ballerina S.D. (Stroud 1989, U.K.) Tube and sepals pale pink, corolla soft lavender. Growth upright and bushy. Medium-sized flowers freely borne. Makes an excellent standard.

Frosted Flame S. (Handley 1975, U.K.) Tube and sepals white, faintly shaded salmon pink, corolla bright flame. Medium to large flowers. Will make a first-class basket plant.

Garden News D. (Handley 1978, U.K.) Tube and sepals pink, corolla cerise. Medium to large flowers freely produced over a long period. Excellent as bush or standard.

Gartenmeister Bondstedt T. (Bondstedt 1905, Germany.) Flowers rich orange. Foliage dark reddish colour. Upright growth. Free flowering for long period.

Gay Fandango S.D. (Nelson 1951, U.S.A.) Tube and sepals rosy-carmine, corolla pinkish magenta. Rather long flowers, excellent grower. Flowers freely.

Golden Anniversary D. (Stubbs 1980, U.S.A.) Tube and sepals white, corolla light purple. The foliage is yellow overlaid with bronze. Ideal for a hanging basket.

'Citation', a good bushy plant with distinctive flowers, in which the corolla consists of spreading recurved segments

Golden Dawn S. (Haag 1951, U.S.A.) Tube and sepals pale salmon, corolla light orange to rose. Very easy to grow, makes ideal standard. Flowers freely produced over long period. Well worth growing.

Golden Marinka F. (Weber 1959, U.S.A.) Tube and sepals red, corolla deep red. Single. Foliage variegated, green and gold with red veining. Sport of 'Marinka'. Excellent basket variety, this cultivar requires more light than most others.

Golden Treasure F. (Carter 1860, U.K.) Tube and sepals scarlet, corolla purple magenta. Foliage variegated green-gold. Self branching and fairly free flowering.

Gracilis Variegata F.S. Tube and sepals scarlet, corolla purple, scarlet at base. Foliage variegated silvery green, purple flushed cerise. Upright. Spreading when grown as a hardy plant, colour of foliage varies considerably, this is where the purple becomes dominant. If grown in greenhouse the colouring is silvery green.

Granada D. (Schnabel 1957, U.S.A.) Tube deep carmine, sepals deep carmine, tipped green, lighter carmine underneath, corolla rich dull purple, splashed carmine. Plant growth is strong and upright, fairly large flowers, produced freely. Has been described as heat resistant and foolproof!

Hampshire Beauty S.D. (Clark 1987, U.K.) Tube and sepals white, corolla pale ice blue. Medium-sized flowers freely borne on superb green and deep yellow variegated foliage. Growth upright and stiff.

Hampshire Blue S.D. (Clark 1983, U.K.) Tube and sepals white, corolla pale powder blue. Medium-sized flowers sometimes single or semi-double, freely produced on bushy but upright growth. Will make an excellent standard.

Happy Fellow S. (Waltz 1965, U.S.A.) Tube and sepals pale orange, corolla smokey orange. Excellent as bush or standard; good for summer bedding.

Harry Gray D. (Dunnett 1981, U.K.) Flowers white tinged with pink. Extremely free flowering, very bushy and easy to grow. Naturally trailing growth ideal for a hanging basket. Superb for exhibition or decoration.

Heidi Ann D. (Smith 1970, U.K.) Tube and sepals crimson, corolla bright lilac, paler at base, veined cerise. Superb small cultivar. Plants grow very bushy, flowering over a long period. Ideal for small greenhouse. (See opposite).

Heinrich Heinkel T. (Rehnelt 1905) Flowers rose red/salmon pink. Very free flowering. Makes low bush, but upright. Foliage dark red.

Henri Poincare S. (Lemoine 1905, France) Tube and sepals red, corolla violet blue. Makes excellent trailer or bush. Free flowering.

Hindu Belle S. (Munkner 1959, U.S.A.) Tube white, sepals white tipped green, flushed pink underneath, corolla rich burgundy. Rather a slow grower, but is worth growing if only because the flowers have a lot of substance, they last for a long time, and are very distinctive.

Howletts Hardy S. (Howlett 1952, U.K.) Tube and sepals scarlet, corolla violet purple, paler at base, veined scarlet. A large flowered cultivar. Flowers freely. Excellent grower.

Iced Champagne S. (Jennings 1968, U.K.) Tube and sepals pink, corolla a paler shade of pink. One that slipped through the net in previous editions. It makes a superb plant in bush or standard form. The flowers are profuse over a long period on good strong upright growth. A first-class show plant.

Igloo Maid D. (Holmes 1972, U.K.) Tube white, sepals white, tipped green, corolla white with faint touch of pink. Very good flowers which show well against the dark foliage.

Indian Maid D. (Waltz 1962, U.S.A.) Tube and sepals red to scarlet, corolla rich purple. Large flowers, produced freely, an easy to grow plant. (See page 46).

Jack Acland S. (Haag 1952, U.S.A.) Tube and sepals bright pink, corolla deep rose, ageing to bright pink. Flowers large and very free. Makes an excellent fan, standard or pyramid.

Kegworth Carnival D. (Smith 1978, U.K.) Tube and sepals ice white, corolla brilliant red. An excellent choice for a hanging basket. The foliage is naturally trailing but quite bushy and flowers are produced freely.

Keystone S. (Haag 1945, U.S.A.) Tube pink, sepals pale pink, tipped green, deeper pink underneath, corolla pale pink. A truly dainty little cultivar. Will produce quite bright pink flowers in profusion. (See page 29).

King's Ransom D. (Schnabel 1954, U.S.A.) Tube and sepals clear white, corolla deep purple. A large well shaped flower. Easy to grow as standard or bush.

Lady Kathleen Spence S. (Ryle 1975, U.K.) Tube white, sepals white tipped green, pale pink underneath, corolla lavender. First class in all aspects. Flowers do not lose form or fade with age. (See page 49).

La Fiesta D. (Kennett 1962, U.S.A.) Tube white, sepals white tipped green, corolla reddish purple, white petaloids splashed cerise. Easy to grow. Makes good bush but will also trail. Flowers freely.

L'Arlesienne S.D. (Colville 1968, U.K.) Tube pink, sepals pink tipped green, corolla white, veined pink, ageing to palest pink. This is a vigorous upright grower. Easy to grow, producing plenty of large blooms.

'Heidi Ann', highly recommended as a small cultivar, with a neat bushy habit and long period of bloom

Lena *S.D.* (Bunney 1862, U.K.)   Tube flesh pink, sepals pale flesh pink, deeper pink underneath, tipped green, corolla purple, becoming paler at base, flushed pink. One of the easiest fuchsias to grow. Hardy. May be grown to any shape. (See page 9).

Lena Dalton *D.* (Reimers 1953, U.S.A.)   Tube pale pink, sepals pale pink, white in shade, corolla blue, ageing to rosy mauve. Very compact growth. Free flowering. Ideal for growing in small pot class at shows.

Leonora S. (Tiret 1960, U.S.A.)   Tube pink, sepals pink tipped green, corolla pink. A good show plant, always makes a nice shaped plant with flowers freely borne.

Linda Goulding S. (Goulding 1981, U.K.)   Tube and sepals pale pink, corolla white. Medium-sized flowers produced in abundance on upright bushy growth. A very attractive plant.

Linhope Sprite S. (Ryle 1975, U.K.)   Tube rose, sepals pink, corolla violet purple with pink base. Medium-sized flowers. Free flowering. Good grower.

Lyes Unique S. (Lye 1868, U.K.)   Tube and sepals white, corolla pinkish orange. Small flowers but freely produced.

Maharaja D. (Castro 1971, U.S.A.)   Tube pinkish, sepals pink tipped green,

Below: 'Indian Maid' has large flowers plentifully borne
Opposite: 'Leonora', a perfect show plant

salmon underneath, corolla purple, splashed salmon and orange. Beautiful flower. Perfect form, makes excellent standard.

Mantilla T. (Reiter 1948) Flowers rich carmine. Foliage bronzy green, narrow leaves. This will make a good vigorous cascade and I have also grown it well as a standard. Very free flowering.

Margaret D. (Wood 1943, U.K.) Tube and sepals carmine, corolla purple, pink at base, veined cerise. Vigorous, tall growing cultivar. Excellent for hardy border. Blooms continually through the summer. May be used as a standard.

Mary T. (Bondstedt 1905) Flowers rich red, even vivid scarlet, set against a narrow leaved bronzy purple foliage. One well worth growing as it flowers over the whole summer.

Mary Lockyer D. (Colville 1967, U.K.) Tube carmine, sepals carmine, tipped green, corolla lilac marbled carmine and pink. A plant which produces plenty of large flowers on a strong upright growth. Does well outside during the summer.

Mission Bells S. (Walker and Jones 1948, U.S.A.) Tube and sepals red, corolla purple, bell shaped. Flowers prolifically. Makes a first rate standard.

Molesworth D. (Lemoine 1903, France) Tube and sepals cerise red, corolla creamy white, veined cerise. Probably the most versatile cultivar, grows well in any shape. Flowers prolifically.

Monta Rosa D. (Colville 1966, U.K.) Tube pink, sepals pink tipped green, corolla white, veined pink. Excellent in every way, good upright growth, yet bushy. Very free flowering.

Morning Light D. (Waltz 1960, U.S.A.) Tube coral pink, sepals white tipped green, pink at base and edge, palest pink underneath, corolla lavender, splashed pale pink and deep pink. Foliage is unusual in that it is golden green with crimson midrib, turns darker with age. An attractive combination of flower colouring and foliage. Makes a good bush or standard, but requires good winter conditions.

My Dear D. (Waltz 1959, U.S.A.) Tube white, sepals white flushed pink at tip, corolla lavender paler at base, ageing to pinkish mauve. A self branching bushy cultivar. Flowers freely produced. Very delicate appearance.

My Fair Lady D. (Colville 1966, U.K.) Tube and sepals strawberry red, corolla lavender, turning reddish, pink at base. Excellent grower. Easy to grow as bush or standard.

Nicola Jane D. (Dawson 1959, U.K.) Tube cerise pink, sepals cerise, tipped green, corolla pale pink flushed and veined cerise. Growth upright, bushy. Excellent as bush or standard. Flowers freely produced. Easy to grow. Hardy.

Normandy Belle S. (Martin 1961, U.S.A.) Tube and sepals white flushed pink, corolla orchid blue. Excellent as standard. Flowers freely.

Olive Jackson S.D. (Handley 1974, U.K.) Tube rose, sepals pale rose tipped green, corolla bluish purple, paling to white at base. A nice compact plant. Flowers freely produced.

Orange Crush S. (Handley 1972, U.K.) Tube orange salmon, sepals orange, corolla bright orange at base. Beautiful orange cultivar. Vigorous grower, needs to be well pinched back when young. Makes a good standard.

Other Fellow S. (Hazard and Hazard 1946, U.S.A.) Tube white, sepals white tipped green, corolla pink, white at base. A little beauty. Very free flowering and easy to grow. Upright but bushy. (See page 10).

Party Frock S.D. (Walker and Jones 1953, U.S.A.) Tube and sepals pale rose,

'Margaret' above, is also suitable for the border; 'Lady Kathleen Spence', below, with shapely long-lasting flowers

corolla lovely pale blue with outer petals soft pink. Good strong grower. Ideal as a standard. Flowers freely.

Peacock *D.* (Dr O. Colville 1981, U.K.)　Tube and sepals scarlet, corolla rich violet blue, making a vivid contrast. Strong upright grower with dark shiny foliage. A showy fuchsia as its name suggests.

Peloria *D.* (Martin 1961, U.S.A.)　Tube darkish red, sepals dark red, corolla purple, the outer petals red some attached to sepals. A strong tall growing cultivar, makes a large bushy plant or standard. Flowers fairly free, these are a striking colour against the medium green foliage.

Pink Flamingo *S.D.* (Fuchsia Forest Castro 1961, U.S.A.)　Tube and sepals dark pink, corolla pale pink. An excellent large flowered, free flowing cascade.

Pink Galore *D.* (Fuchsia La 1958, U.S.A.)　Tube pink, sepals pink tipped green, corolla pale rose pink. Not too easy to grow, but will make a good basket if two or three plants are used. Flowers are produced very freely.

Pink Marshmallow *D.* (Stubbs 1971, U.S.A.)　Tube pale pink to white, sepals white tipped green, blushed pink underneath, corolla white, flushed and veined pale pink. This is possibly the largest cultivar produced. Very easy to grow. Flowers freely produced in spite of its size. Makes an excellent trailer. (See page 19).

Pink Quartet *S.D.* (Walker and Jones 1949, U.S.A.)　Pink flowers. Tube and sepals deeper pink, corolla pale pink. Flowers medium to large. Strong grower. Makes an excellent standard. Free flowering.

President *F.* (Standish 1841, U.K.)　Tube and sepals bright red, corolla reddish cerise, scarlet at base. Single. Foliage dark green, tinged red. Vigorous grower and free flowering. Foliage colour best when grown outdoors, and often semi-double.

President Margaret Slater *S.* (Taylor 1973, U.K.)　Tube white, sepals white flushed pink, tipped green, salmon pink under, corolla pinkish mauve, salmon mauve in the sun, paler at base. Makes a superb basket, neat foliage which well covers the basket. Flowers prolifically over a long period.

Princess Dollar *D.* (Lemoine 1912, France)　Tube and sepals cerise, corolla deep purple. Growth upright, bushy, is also hardy. This plant is found in every florist's or market. Very easy to grow. Flowers without fail throughout the summer. (See page 18).

Quasar *D.* (Walker 1974, U.S.A.)　Tube and sepals white, corolla mid-blue. Large flowers freely produced on strong upright growth.

Red Ribbon *D.* (Martin 1959, U.S.A.)　Tube and sepals red, corolla white. This cultivar may be grown in all forms, including trailer. Very free flowering and easy to grow. Makes a good substitute for 'Texas Longhorn' and much more reliable in all ways.

Red Shadows *D.* (Waltz 1962, U.S.A.)　Tube and sepals red, corolla deep purple, wide opening, with petals lightly flushed scarlet. A very attractive cultivar. Free flowering.

Red Spider *S.* (Reiter 1946, U.S.A.)　Tube and sepals deep crimson red, corolla darker rose. Flowers long, freely produced, trailing growth.

Rev. Doctor Brown *D.* (Taylor 1973, U.K.)　Tube palest pink, sepals pale pink, tipped green, deeper pink underneath, corolla white, veined pink. A self branching free flowering cultivar, makes a strong bushy plant. Easy to grow.

Ridestar *D.* (Blackwell 1965, U.K.)　Tube and sepals scarlet, corolla deep lavender blue, ageing to rosy lavender pink at base. A vigorous growing, self branching cultivar. Makes excellent bush or standard. Flowers profusely over long period.

Rosecroft Beauty F. (Eden 1969, U.K.) Tube and sepals crimson, corolla white, flushed and veined cerise. Foliage pale green, edged cream and cerise. Growth upright but bushy. This is a sport from 'Snowcap'.

Rose of Castille S. (Banks 1869, U.K.) Tube greenish white, sepals white flushed very pale pink, tipped green, corolla purple, flushed rose, white flash in centre and base of petals. A super small-flowered cultivar, easy to grow as standard or bush.

Rose of Castille Improved S. (Lane 1871, U.K.) Tube pale pink, sepals flesh pink tipped green, corolla violet, veined deep pink, ageing to reddish purple. Medium sized flowers on strong growing plant.

Royal Velvet D. (Waltz 1962, U.S.A.) Tube and sepals crimson, corolla deep purple, splashed crimson. One of the best in this colour range. Makes a good show plant. Good standard. Flowers very freely.

Rufus the Red S. (Nelson 1952, U.S.A.) Flowers turkey red, medium sized, produced very freely. Strong grower. Excellent as a standard. (See page 21).

Samson F. (Peterson Fuchsia Farms 1957, U.S.A.) Tube pink, sepals pink, paler at tip and turning to green, deep pink underneath, corolla purple, fading to pink at base, deep pink veins. Double. Foliage variegated pale green and yellow. Growth cascade. One of the most vigorous with variegated leaves, blooms freely. Excellent greenhouse cultivar.

Shy Lady D. (Waltz 1955, U.S.A.) Tube white, sepals white tipped green, corolla white, tinted pink. Growth bushy so needs little pinching to make a good plant. Certainly not shy when flowering.

Sincerety D. (Holmes 1968, U.K.) Tube pale pinkish white or greenish white, sepals white with touch of pink at base and underneath, corolla white or creamy white depending on growing conditions. An excellent white flowered fuchsia. Makes good plant indoors, but also does well outside for summer bedding. Growth straight and vigorous. Flowers freely. (See page 55).

Sleigh Bells S. (Schnabel 1954.) Large all white flowers, probably the best white cultivar. Excellent as a standard. Very free flowering.

Snowcap S.D. (Henderson, U.K.) Tube and sepals red, corolla white, veined cerise. Medium sized flowers, freely produced. Good as a standard. Also stands well outdoors during summer.

Sophisticated Lady D. (Martin 1964, U.S.A.) Tube pink, sepals pink, paler towards tip than green, corolla creamy white. Quite good for baskets, will also make quite a good bush plant.

Southgate D. (Walker and Jones 1951, U.S.A.) Tube pinkish green, sepals pale pink, tipped green, deeper pink on underside, corolla pale pink, flushed and veined deeper pink. A very good double pink. Easy to grow as bush or standard. Flowers freely.

Strawberry Delight F. (Gadsby 1970, U.K.) Tube and sepals crimson, corolla white, flushed pink and heavily veined. Double. Foliage yellowish green and bronze becoming green with age. Growth trailing. Beautiful foliage with the added attraction of brightly coloured flowers. Easy to grow. Requires a little more feeding for continuous growth and flower.

Strawberry Sundae D. (Kennett 1961, U.S.A.) Tube greenish white, sepals white tipped green, corolla lilac pink. A good trailer, rather striking with the dark green foliage. Requires greenhouse conditions for best results. Flowers freely.

Sunray F. (Milne 1872, U.K.)   Tube scarlet, sepals deep pink, lighter at tip, scarlet underneath, corolla cerise purple. Single. Foliage pale green edged creamy white, flushed cerise. Growth upright and bushy. Prefers a smaller pot than most, also needs carefully watering.

Susan Ford D. (Clyne 1974, U.K.)   Tube deep rose pink, sepals deep rose pink, lighter pink underneath, corolla lavender rose at base. Vigorous self branching fuchsia, makes a tall bushy plant. Free flowering. The corolla stays closed.

Swanley Gem S. (Cannell 1901, U.K.)   Tube and sepals scarlet, corolla purple, pale scarlet at base, veined scarlet. Upright yet bushy, lovely in every respect. Flowers small but freely produced. Ideal for showing. Corolla opens almost flat.

Sweet Leilani D. (Tiret 1957, U.S.A.)   Tube and sepals pale pink, corolla pale smoky blue with serrated edge. Flowers large and freely produced. An excellent grower as bush or standard.

Swingtime D. (Tiret 1950, U.S.A.)   Tube and sepals rich red, corolla white, faintly veined with red. Flowers large: one of the best in the colour range. Good as bush, standard or pyramid. Easy to grow. Free flowering. (See page 6).

S'wonderful D. (Fuchsia Forest Castro 1961, U.S.A.)   Tube and sepals pink, corolla inner petals lavender, outer orchid pink. Semi-trailer. Free flowering.

Sunset S. (Niederholtzer 1938, U.S.A.)   Tube pink, sepals pink tipped green, bright salmon pink underneath, corolla orange cerise. If this plant is grown as a standard it really deserves its name. Self branching and easy to grow.

Television D. (Evans 1950, U.K.)   Tube white, sepals white, tipped green, corolla deep lavender blue. Excellent grower, free flowering. Good as bush or standard.

Temptation S. (Peterson 1959, U.S.A.)   Tube white, sepals white and long, corolla orange rose. Good branching habit. Free flowering. Makes a good standard.

'Thalia', a vigorous and free-flowering fuchsia

Tennessee Waltz *D.* (Walker and Jones 1951, U.S.A.) Tube and sepals rose madder, corolla mauve flushed rose. Very free flowering. One of the easiest to grow as bush or standard, good for the beginners. Makes outstanding plant in a short time. Could also be grown as pillar or pyramid. (See pages 11 and 58).

Texas Longhorn *S.D.* (Fuchsia L.A. 1968, U.S.A.) Tube and sepals scarlet, corolla white, veined cerise. Most people try to grow this cultivar because of its long and large flowers, but it is difficult to grow. Requires more feeding than most.

Thalia *T.* (Turner 1855) Flowers bright orange, set against a red-bronze foliage. Upright grower and very free flowering. (See opposite).

The Aristocrat *D.* (Waltz 1953, U.S.A.) Tube and sepals pale rose pink, corolla creamy white, veined pale rose at base. Flowers large, very free for size of bloom, corolla serrated. Growth upright, makes excellent standard. Easy to grow.

Theroigne de Merricourt *D.* (Lemoine 1903, France) Tube and sepals crimson, corolla creamy white, veined cerise at base. Multi-sepaled double. An outstanding cultivar, both for size and substance of the individual bloom, freely produced. Easy to grow, requires pinching early for good results.

The Small Woman *F.* (Wagtails 1969, U.K.) Tube pale pink, sepals pink tipped green, corolla lilac pink. Double. Foliage green splashed gold. Growth trailing. A sport from 'Lovable'. Not easy to grow but when flowers open it is quite outstanding.

Thunderbird *D.* (Tiret 1957, U.S.A.) Tube and sepals neyron rose, corolla vermilion to china rose. A most elegant flower. Does not make too large a plant, so requires smaller pot than most. Two or three plants in basket will make a free branching, free flowering group.

Tolling Bell *S.* (Turner 1964, U.K.) Short thick scarlet tube and sepals, corolla white, veined cerise. A perfect bell shaped flower. A vigorous grower, but makes a well shaped plant with early pinching. Good as a standard.

Trail Blazer *D.* (Reiten 1951, U.S.A.) Tube and sepals crimson, corolla rosy purple. A strong self branching trailer. Flowers profusely over long period. Can be grown in other forms with staking. (See page 32).

Trase *S.D.* (Dawson 1959, U.K.) Tube and sepals crimson, corolla white, veined and flushed carmine. Growth upright and bushy. One of the best hardy fuchsias. Very free flowering and easy to grow. (See page 14).

Traudchen Bondstedt *T.* (Bondstedt 1905, Germany.) Flowers pale salmon pink. Foliage pale green. Will flower fairly freely.

Tricolor. *F.* Tube and sepals crimson, corolla purple, cerise at base. Single. Foliage variegated, cream and green, flushed red. Growth upright and bushy, hardy. This is lower growing than 'Gracilis Variegata', and flowers later.

Tristesse *D.* (Blackwell 1965, U.K.) Tube pale rose pink, sepals rose pink, tipped green, corolla pale lilac blue. Makes a low bushy plant which will flower freely. Ideal for the small greenhouse or bedding during the summer.

Tropic Sunset *F.* (Antonelli 1964, U.S.A.) Tube and sepals carmine, corolla purple, splashed pink. Double. Foliage reddish bronze, small. Growth cascade and self branching. Although vigorous, it is very free flowering, and makes a shapely plant.

Trumpeter *T.* (Reiter 1946). Flowers pale geranium lake. Foliage bluish green. Makes a bushy cascading plant, not overlarge. Flowers freely.

Uncle Charlie *S.D.* (Tiret 1949, U.S.A.) Tube and sepals red, corolla lavender blue. Large free flowering. Upright but bushy growth.

Vanessa Jackson *S.* (Handley 1980, U.K.) Tube salmon-red, sepals long, salmon-orange, corolla salmon-orange shading to orange-red, then cardinal red at edges. Large trumpet-shaped flowers with flared petal edges resembling a daffodil. A prolific-flowering cascade fuchsia.

Voodoo *D.* (Tiret 1952, U.S.A.) Tube and sepals dark red, corolla dark purplish violet. A striking colour. Largish flowers, freely produced on upright, yet bushy growth. Makes good standard as well as bush.

Warpaint *D.* (Kennett 1960, U.S.A.) Tube greenish white, sepals white, pink underneath, corolla cerise purple, splashed pink, ageing to light purple. Growth upright; makes a dense spreading plant. Rather short jointed between leaf nodes so tends to hide its flowers, which are borne freely. Grow in a light position.

Wave of Life *F.* (Henderson 1869, U.K.) Tube and sepals scarlet, corolla reddish purple. Single. Foliage golden with pink stems. Growth training. A small cascading type with attractive foliage. (See opposite).

White Gold *F.* (Yorke 1953) Tube pinky white, sepals white, pink at base, green tip, corolla white veined pale pink. Single, the petals are of unequal size. Foliage golden, goes green with age. Growth rather lax, self branching. Grows rather slowly but is really beautiful if well grown. Avoid getting spots of water on foliage.

White Spider *S.* (Haag 1951, U.S.A.) Tube and sepals soft pink, corolla white. Neat bushy plant. Flowers freely, good for baskets.

Wings of Song *D.* (Blackwell 1968, U.K.) Tube and sepals bright rose pink, corolla lavender pink, veined pink. A vigorous growing, free flowering trailing or bush plant.

Winifred *S.* (Chatfield 1973, U.K.) Tube pale pink, sepals deep rose pink, salmon pink underneath, corolla cerise pink, pale pink at base. A vigorous grower, requires quite a lote of pinching. Flowers freely. Excellent for summer bedding.

Winston Churchill *D.* (Garson 1942, U.S.A.) Tube pink, sepals pink, tipped green, bright pink underneath, corolla lavender blue, ageing to pale purple, splashed and veined pink. Splendid small bushy fuchsia. Ideal for small greenhouse, makes a very neat bush or half standard. Flowers profusely.

Yankee Clipper *D.* (Soo Yun Field 1971, U.S.A.) Tube crimson, sepals crimson, scarlet underneath, tipped green, corolla rich ruby red, splashed scarlet. A very eye-catching cultivar. Will make a large plant fairly easily. Growth upright. Flowers freely.

'Sincerity', above, one of the finest white fuchsias; 'Wave of Life', below, has the added bonus of attractive leaves

Pests

The most troublesome pests of fuchsias are aphids, glasshouse whitefly and glasshouse red spider mite. These mainly affect plants growing in greenhouses or in houses but during the summer they may also infest plants growing out of doors. Other pests that are sometimes a nuisance include capsid bugs and caterpillars.

Aphids of various different species establish colonies on young shoots, on the undersides of leaves and on flower buds. They feed on the sap and excrete a sticky, sugary substance, known as honeydew, which makes the foliage sticky and encourages the growth of unsightly, black, sooty moulds.

Glasshouse whitefly has a similar effect. The young whiteflies are pale, whitish green or yellow, flat, oval scales, up to about 1.5 mm long. They feed on the undersides of the leaves and eventually adults emerge from them. These are small, pure white, winged insects which look like minute months. They tend to congregate on the younger leaves, where they lay eggs, and if they are disturbed they fly briefly before resettling on the plants. Both the young and adult whiteflies excrete a lot of honeydew and cause extensive fouling of the foliage of infested plants. Breeding is virtually continuous in glasshouses where the relatively high temperatures favour them.

Glasshouse red spider mites also live on the undersides of the leaves. Colonies containing vast numbers of these microscopic mites are often established and populations increase very rapidly, especially in relatively dry, hot conditions. Young and adult mites feed on leaf tissues and the first symptoms of attack usually show as localised areas of light discoloration on the upper leaf surfaces. Later the leaves may turn yellow, then brown and finally drop from the plant prematurely. When mite populations are high they may be seen swarming over infested plants on a fine silk webbing which they spin.

Capsid bugs are generally more troublesome on plants growing out of doors but may also damage plants in glasshouses. The bugs pierce the young tissues to feed on the sap and some days or weeks after they have fed the leaves and flowers that have developed show a characteristic pattern of irregular, tattered holes and distorted growth. This is caused by a toxin injected into the tissues by these bugs and in some cases this may kill growing points and cause flower buds to abort.

Caterpillars of various species of moth may be found on fuchsias from time to time. One of the largest, and most alarming, is the caterpillar of the elephant hawk moth. This grows to a length of almost 3 inches (7.5cm) and its appearance when full grown, is rather startling. The segments of the body just behind the head bear two pairs of conspicuous eye-like markings and at the dark brown end of the rear body there is a horn-like projection.

Control

Chemical control of pests is not always easy or effective. Every effort should therefore be made to ensure that plants are free from pests when they are first brought into a house or a glasshouse. If possible glasshouses should be cleared of plants during the autumn or winter and washed down thoroughly. The key to successful control of pests on fuchsias is to keep a close watch on plants for the first indications of trouble and the main objective should be to eliminate pests before they become established.

Individual fuchsia plants growing in pots may be fumigated by enclosing them for about half an hour in a large polythene bag containing a dichlorvos plastic strip (Vapona pest strip). This will kill most of the aphids, whiteflies, red spider mites, capsids or caterpillars that may be present and the treatment can be repeated after about a week, if necessary.

Some insecticides can damage fuchsias, especially the flowers, and so spraying should be done with caution. Plants should be treated in the evening or on cool cloudy days and, if necessary, the plants should be watered before treatment.

The two most persistent and troublesome pests are whitefly and red spider mite. The former can be controlled by spraying with permethrin, bioresmethrin or pyrethrum. Only the adult stage is readily killed by insecticides and so heavy infestations may require treatment every 3 or 4 days for several weeks. Red spider mite can be controlled by spraying thoroughly with malathion or pirimiphos-methyl at 7-day intervals until the pest is controlled. As an alternative to using chemicals these two pests can be controlled respectively by a parasitic wasp, *Encarsia formosa*, and a predatory mite, *Phytoseiulus persimilis*. These beneficial animals are only effective during the summer as they require high temperatures. Aphids, capsids and caterpillars can be controlled by using any of the insecticides mentioned above, although hand picking is usually adequate to deal with caterpillars.

Fuchsias grown out of doors are less susceptible to attack by pests than are those grown under glass. Aphids and capsid bugs are the main problem in the garden and they can be dealt with as described above.

'Tennessee Waltz', an outstanding fuchsia which may be grown as a bush or trained as a standard, pillar or pyramid

Diseases

Very few diseases of fuchsias have been recorded in Great Britain. Those occurring most frequently are described on the next pages.

Black Root Rot (Thielaviopsis basicola)

Fuchsias grown in unsterilized compost are susceptible to this trouble, which is caused by a soil-borne fungus. The roots become black and rotten with the result that the leaves become discoloured, but they do not necessarily fall.

Control. This disease can only be confirmed by microscopic examination of diseased roots. If it is suspected, however, that plants have been affected by this disease, the roots should be washed and any which are dead or bear black patches should be cut off and burnt. The plants should be repotted in sterile compost and then watered two or three times at three-weekly intervals with a solution of 1 oz of captan (50 per cent wettable powder), in 2½ gals. of water (28g/11 litres) or drenched with benomyl, carbendazim or thiophanate-methyl according to the manufacturers instructions. It will also be worth while to spray affected plants with a foliar feed to boost their vigour and encourage the development of new roots.

Fuchsia Rust (Pucciniastrum epilobii)

This disease, which sometimes occurs on greenhouse plants, shows first as pale orange powdery pustules on yellow or reddish spots, predominantly on the lower leaf surfaces. Later, brownish pustules appear, also on the under surfaces. This rust fungus, however, is found most frequently on willow-herbs, and these weeds, therefore, should not be allowed to grow in the vicinity of fuchsias. Most new infections in greenhouses arise from buying diseased plants.

Control. Diseased leaves should be removed and burnt. The plants should then be sprayed several times at about fortnightly intervals, with maneb, thiram or zineb, or preferably propiconazole.

Grey Mould (Botrytis cinerea)

This fungus may cause rotting of the flowers, and in severe cases can affect the leaves and also shoots, causing die back. The affected tissues become covered with a greyish mass of spores.

Control. This disease is only likely to be troublesome where the atmosphere is very humid, and can usually be controlled by careful ventilation and removal of dead and dying flowers and leaves. If the trouble persists, the plants should be sprayed with benomyl, carbendazim or thiophanate-methyl, but regular use of any of these could lead to the development of resistant strains of the fungus, so they cease to be effective. Alternatively use captan or thiram or, better still, fumigate the greenhouse with tecnazene (TCNB) smokes.

Physiological Disorders.

Fuchsia leaves frequently become discoloured and fall prematurely as a result of unsuitable cultural conditions. Great fluctuations in temperature can cause purpling of the leaves, whereas yellowing or brown blotching is usually due to too wet or too dry soil conditions. Malnutrition can cause a discoloration of the foliage but the leaves may not fall. Sudden and severe symptoms frequently occur as a result of chemical injury, and as fuchsias are damaged by several different insecticides and fungicides, all chemicals should be used with care and according to the manufacturer's instructions.

Severe leaf fall does not necessarily lead to the death of a plant. It may shoot again in due course, but it can be cut back or cuttings can be taken from it. Once new leaves have appeared, these should be sprayed with a foliar feed to make the plant more vigorous.

Growing fuchsias outdoors

Most fuchsias are not hardy enough to survive the winters outside in most parts of Britain. But in the southwest of England and the west of Scotland, where the winters are milder, fuchsias do survive with little trouble. These are chiefly *Fuchsia magellanica*, its cultivar 'Riccartonii' and variety *molinae*.

Fuchsias are very useful in the garden, being at their best in late summer and early autumn, when gardens sometimes begin to look rather drab. They will do well in many situations, in mixed borders, tubs and so on, being adaptable plants, growing in a variety of conditions.

Fuchsias are also used for planting out in the summer, being taken up again before the frosts and overwintered in a frost-free place. This does involve extra work for the gardener, and a less troublesome way of growing fuchsias outside is to choose hardy cultivars which should survive the winter without protection. There is not such a wide choice of cultivars as for indoor kinds, but there is nevertheless a reasonable selection.

It is difficult to predict the hardiness of various plants, so much depends on how the plant is grown, and on the micro-climate of the garden. Among the factors which will help a plant to survive the winter are a position in sun and a well-drained soil. Both of these factors promote the ripening of the shoots in late summer and early autumn, making the tissues better able to resist freezing at low temperatures.

So, for plants that are to be grown entirely outdoors it is essential to choose the hardier cultivars (a list is given on pp. 63–64). When planting from pots make sure that the lower part of the stem (at least four inches) is buried below ground level. This ensures that several growth buds are protected from frost during the winter and these will produce new flowering shoots in the following summer. Some protection can be given round the base of the stem during winter, using bracken or straw or leaf-mould.

In spring the plants are pruned back, each branch being cut to within one or two pairs of buds at its base. It is important that this pruning is left until spring, because if it is done earlier, water from winter rains may easily collect on the cut surfaces and start rotting in the stems.

HARDY CULTIVARS

The following have received awards from the RHS after two trials in the garden at Wisley, but other hardy cvs. are included in the list on pp. 37–54.

Abundance (Neiderholtzer 1944) (19–21 in: 50–55cm). Single. Tube glossy red, sepals same glossy red but slightly darker, corolla velvety purple changing to red at base with veining. Foliage dark green, veins, midrib and margins purple. Vigorous grower, erect and arching. Free flowering.

Achievement (See page 37).

Bashful (Tabraham U.K.) (1½–2 feet: 45–60cm). Double. Tube red, sepals slightly deeper red, corolla white flushed red. Growth vigorous but compact, small leaves. Very free flowering.

Blue Bonnet (Tabraham U.K.) (15–24 in: 40–60cm). Double. Tube and sepals red, corolla violet overlaid with paler violet, red under midrib. Growth compact, inclined to spread. Free flowering.

Brilliant (Bull 1865). (1½ feet: 45cm). Large single flowers. Tube and sepals cerise, recurving, corolla violet magenta. Vigorous and bushy growth. Free flowering.

Chillerton Beauty (Bass 1847, U.K.) (24–26 in: 60–66cm). Tube pale pink, sepals pale pink, tipped green, deeper pink underneath, corolla purple (ageing to rosy purple), veined pink. Easy growing, free flowering cultivar for garden or greenhouse. Makes large standard or bush. (See page 29).

C.J. Howlett (Howlett, U.K.) (1½–2 feet: 40–60cm). Semi-double. Tube scarlet, sepals scarlet tipped green, corolla light cerise, mauve pink at base. The corolla is in two tiers. Easy to grow. Very free to branch and flower.

Cliffs Hardy (Gadsby, U.K.) (24–26 in: 60–65cm). Single. Tube and sepals red, corolla purple, tinged at base red. Growth vigorous, compact and erect. Very free flowering. (See page 15).

Doctor Foster (2½–3 feet: 75–90cm). Large single flowers. Tube and sepals blood red, corolla purple veined scarlet. Slightly spreading habit.

Enfante Prodigue (Prodigy) (Lemoine 1887, France) (4 feet: 1.2m). Semi-double flowers. Tube and sepals carmine, corolla purple. Upright bushy growth.

Eva Boerg (Yorke 1943) (2–2½ feet: 60–75cm). Single flowers. Tube and sepals blush white, corolla violet purple. Arching habit. (See also pages 35 and 40).

Gracilis Variegata (2 feet: 60cm). Variegated leaves, broadly margined cream. A cultivar of *F. magellanica*. (See also page 44).

Graf Witte (Lemoine 1899) (26–31 in: 65–80cm). Tube and sepals carmine, corolla purple veined carmine. Not a tall grower, but covers a lot of ground, makes a very graceful plant. Flowers freely.

Happy (Tabraham 1976, U.K.) (1 foot: 30 cm). Tube and sepals carmine, corolla purple, pink at base, veined carmine. Small flowered cultivar. A very neat compact plant. All flowers look upwards, very free flowering.

Lady Thumb (Roe 1967, U.K.) (20 in: 50cm). Semi-double. Tube and sepals carmine pink, corolla white, veined pink. This is a sport from 'Tom Thumb'. A lovely bushy small plant. Free flowering, good for table standard. (See page 11).

'Gracilis', a tall-growing free-flowering cultivar of *Fuchsia magellanica*

Lena (Bunney 1862) (2 feet: 60cm). Semi-double flowers. Tube and sepals flesh-coloured, corolla purple. Compact, arching growth. (See also pages 9 and 45).

Madame Cornelissen (Cornelissen 1860) (4 feet: 1.2m). Semi-double flowers; tube and sepals rich crimson, corolla white. Tall upright habit.

Magellanica Gracilis (4–4½ feet: 1.2–1.4m). Tube and sepals crimson, corolla purple. Growth pendulous, will grow quite tall. Very free flowering. (See page 62).

Margaret (Wood 1937, U.K.) (4–4½ feet: 1.3–1.4m). Single flowers. Tube and sepals crimson, corolla violet purple with red veining. Vigorous. Free flowering.

Monsieur Thibaud (Lemoine 1898, France) (2–2½ feet: 60–85cm). Single. Tube and sepals cherry pink, corolla lilac. Spreading growth. Free flowering.

Mrs Popple (Elliot 1899, U.K.) (4 feet: 1.2m). Single flowers. Tube and sepals scarlet, corolla deep purple. Vigorous, spreading and trailing habit. Flowers freely produced over long period.

Mrs W. P. Wood (Wood 1949, U.K.) (2–2½ feet: 60–75cm). Single. Tube and sepals flesh pink, recurved, corolla white. Vigorous upright growth. Small but prolific flowers.

Nicola Jane (See page 48).

Peewee Rose (Niederholtzer 1939, U.S.A.) (1½ feet: 45cm). Tube and sepals rose red, corolla red. Single. Grows rather too fast for indoors, but makes a good border plant. Free flowering. Plant in front of border as foliage tends to trail. (See page 12)

Prelude (Kennet and Ross 1958.) (2½ feet: 75cm). Double. Tube and sepals crimson, corolla violet purple. Slightly spreading growth. (See page 28).

Riccartonii (Young 1833, U.K.) (4 feet: 1.2m). Single. Tube and sepals scarlet, corolla dark purple. Strong growing. Free flowering.

Rufus the Red (See pages 21 and 51).

Ruth (Wood, U.K.) (2–2¼ feet: 61–71cm). Single. Tube and sepals pale red, corolla purple, paler at base, veined red. Growth compact and arching. Leaves large. Flowers profusely.

Sealand Prince (5 feet: 1.7m). Sepals rose madder with cream tips, corolla dark violet. Very free flowering.

Thompsonii (Thompson 1840). (2 feet: 60 cm). Single. Tube and sepals bright scarlet, corolla purple. A cultivar of F. *magellanica*.

The British Fuchsia Society was formed to encourage the cultivation of fuchsias, and holds shows throughout the country. Further information about the Society may be obtained from the Honorary Secretary, 29, Princes Crescent, Dollar, Clackmannanshire.